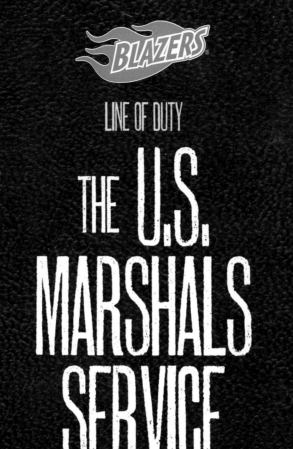

LINE OF DUTY

THE U.S. MARSHALS SERVICE
CATCHING FUGITIVES

by Connie Colwell Miller

Reading Consultant
Barbara J. Fox
Reading Specialist
North Carolina State University

Content Consultant
Kenneth E. deGraffenreid
Professor of Intelligence Studies
Institute of World Politics
Washington, D.C.

Capstone
press

Mankato, Minnesota

Blazers is published by Capstone Press,
151 Good Counsel Drive, P.O. Box 669, Mankato, Minnesota 56002.
www.capstonepress.com

Library of Congress Cataloging-in-Publication Data
Miller, Connie Colwell, 1976–
     The U.S. Marshals Service: catching fugitives / by Connie Colwell Miller.
     p. cm. — (Blazers. Line of duty)
     Summary: "Describes the U.S. Marshals and their role in finding and
arresting fugitives" — Provided by publisher.
     Includes bibliographical references and index.
     ISBN–13: 978-1-4296-1277-7 (hardcover)
     ISBN–10: 1-4296-1277-0 (hardcover)
     1. United States marshals — History — Juvenile literature. I. Title.
II. Series.
HV8144.M37M55 2008
363.28'20973 — dc22   2007028835

Editorial Credits
Aaron Sautter, editor; Bobbi J. Wyss, designer; Wanda Winch, photo researcher

Photo Credits
AP Images/Chuck Burton, 23; Duluth News Tribune/Clint Austin, 25;
     The Herald-Dispatch/Randy Snyder, 8–9; Rogelio V. Solis, 16–17;
     Terry Renna, 18–19
Corbis/Bettmann, 12–13
Getty Images Inc./David McNew, 14; Mario Tama, 6–7; Scott Olson, 20–21
U.S. Marshals Service, cover, 4–5, 11, 22, 26–27; Mai Photo News Agency, Inc./
     Greg Mathieson, 28–29

1 2 3 4 5 6 13 12 11 10 09 08

TABLE OF CONTENTS

HUNTING DOWN CRIMINALS

A criminal **suspect** is on the run from the law. But he won't get far. The U.S. Marshals will hunt him down and take him to jail.

[**suspect** — someone thought to be guilty of a crime]

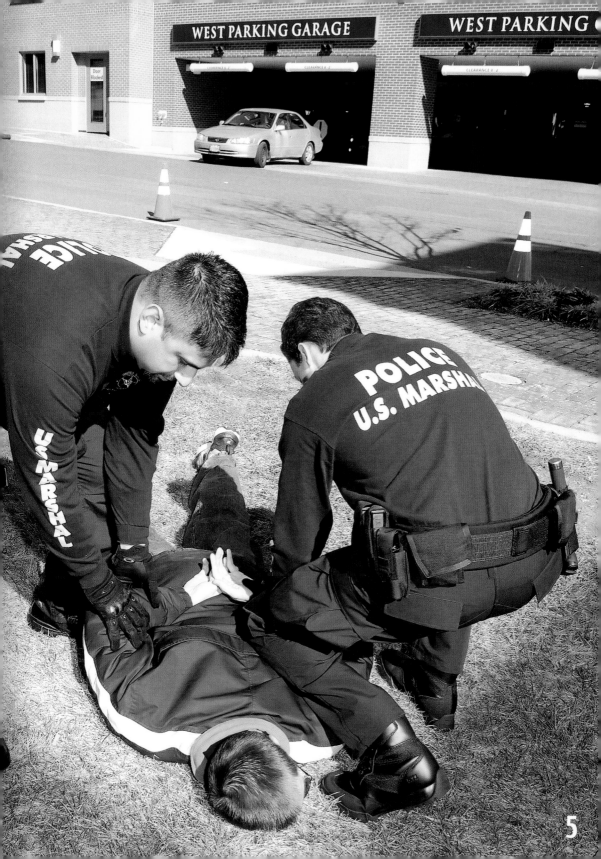

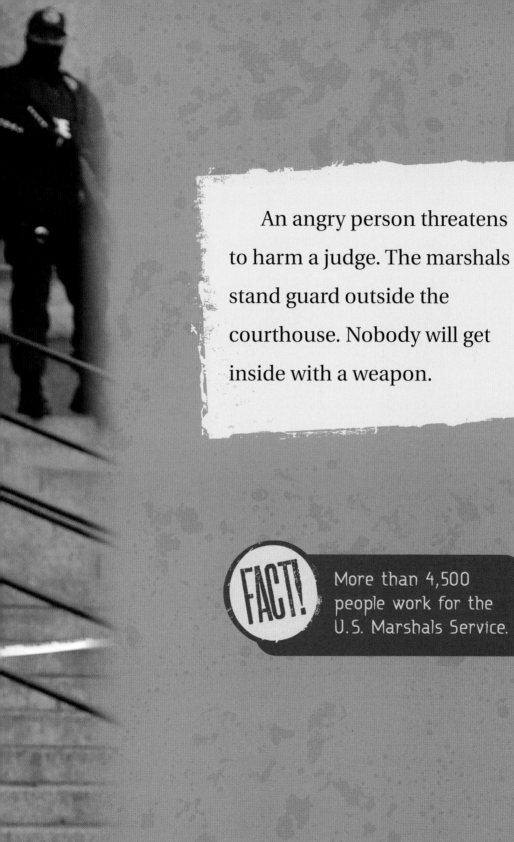

An angry person threatens to harm a judge. The marshals stand guard outside the courthouse. Nobody will get inside with a weapon.

FACT! More than 4,500 people work for the U.S. Marshals Service.

A prisoner is on his way to jail. He can forget about trying to escape. The U.S. Marshals are there to keep him locked up.

FACT! In 2006, U.S. Marshals helped arrest about 85,000 criminals.

Marshals use handcuffs and chains to keep prisoners from trying to escape.

MARSHALS ON DUTY

The U.S. Marshals Service is the oldest **law enforcement** agency in the country. Marshals have many jobs. They hunt down suspects who run from the law.

[**law enforcement** — making sure laws are followed]

This statue honors marshals of the Old West at the U.S. Marshals headquarters in Washington, D.C.

Witnesses in the WSP need to cover their faces in courtrooms.

Marshals place people in the **Witness** Security Program (WSP). This program helps people hide from dangerous criminals.

[**witness** — someone who knows something about a criminal case]

Since 1971, the WSP has helped protect more than 17,600 people.

U.S. Marshals keep **federal** courtrooms safe. Angry people may try to hurt judges or jury members. The marshals stop the criminals before they can hurt anyone.

[**federal** — part of the central government]

FACT! The U.S. Marshals protect more than 2,000 judges.

Marshals make sure prisoners don't escape during transport.

Marshals **transport** prisoners to jail, court, or the hospital. It is the marshals' job to get them there safely.

[**transport** — to take someone from one place to another]

WEAPONS, GEAR, AND VEHICLES

Marshals use many kinds of weapons. They use handguns, shotguns, rifles, and machine guns.

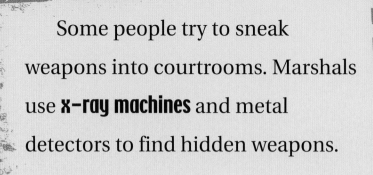

Some people try to sneak weapons into courtrooms. Marshals use **x-ray machines** and metal detectors to find hidden weapons.

[**x-ray machine** — a machine that takes pictures of objects inside bags and suitcases]

The U.S. Marshals Service guards more than 400 U.S. courthouses.

ALL BAGS MUST BE PLACED ON CONVEYER BELT

ALL VISITORS SHALL PRESENT PHOTO I.D. UPON ENTRANCE

UNITED STATES MARSHAL

Marshals use many vehicles to transport prisoners. Marshals use cars or vans for short trips. They take prisoners on airplanes for long trips.

FACT! The U.S. Marshals Service transports about 350,000 prisoners each year.

KEEPING PEOPLE SAFE

Dangerous criminals are the main target of U.S. Marshals. The marshals work hard to find these people and **arrest** them.

[**arrest** — to capture and hold someone for breaking the law]

Marshals work to guard prisoners and keep them in jail. Prisoners who escape might hurt or kill others.

Each day, U.S. Marshals guard more than 55,000 prisoners. Prisoners are held in local jails until their trials are finished in court.

The U.S. Marshals
Service works hard to protect
the United States. Criminals
can't hide for long with U.S.
Marshals on the job.

GLOSSARY

agency (AY-juhn-see) — a government office that provides a service to the country

arrest (uh-REST) — to capture and hold someone for breaking the law

federal (FED-ur-uhl) — part of the central government

jury (JU-ree) — a group of people at a trial that decides if someone is guilty of a crime

law enforcement (LAW en-FORSS-muhnt) — making sure laws are followed

suspect (SUHSS-pekt) — a person believed to be responsible for a crime

transport (transs-PORT) — to move or carry something or someone from one place to another

witness (WIT-niss) — someone who has seen or heard something about a criminal case

x-ray machine (EKS-ray muh-SHEEN) — a machine that takes pictures of solid objects inside bags and suitcases

READ MORE

Broyles, Matthew. *U.S. Air Marshals.* Extreme Careers. New York: Rosen, 2007.

Donovan, Sandra. *Protecting America: A Look at the People Who Keep Our Country Safe.* How Government Works. Minneapolis: Lerner, 2004.

INTERNET SITES

FactHound offers a safe, fun way to find Internet sites related to this book. All of the sites on FactHound have been researched by our staff.

Here's how:
1. Visit *www.facthound.com*
2. Choose your grade level.
3. Type in this book ID **1429612770** for age-appropriate sites. You may also browse subjects by clicking on letters, or by clicking on pictures and words.
4. Click on the **Fetch It** button.

FactHound will fetch the best sites for you!

INDEX